MEDITATIONS FOR MUSICIANS

AMY DUNKER

Batuta Press

MEDITATIONS FOR MUSICIANS

AMY DUNKER

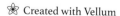

To My Students Past, Present and Future

INTRODUCTION

The musical life is a life in pursuit of perfection. Unfortunately, perfection is elusive; and yet, we continue because that is our nature. While this never-ending pursuit creates great works of art and unforgettable musical moments for both musician and audience, it can come at a high price both physically and emotionally.

The following meditations reflect the knowledge gained in a lengthy career as a performer, composer and teacher. The meditations are short. There are no lengthy explanations. They are meant for the reader to spend time contemplating what the meaning is for them personally and musically. Select one or two and spend a day, a week, a month reflecting on them.

1

Love > Fear

2

Auditions

How did it go?
I didn't play as well as I should have.

Will I get the job?
Maybe

Will this end my career?
Only if you let it.

Is this a failure?
Only if you don't learn anything from it

How did it go?
I played horribly!

Will I get the job?
Probably Not

Will this end my career?
Only if you let it.

Is this a failure?
Only if you don't learn anything from it.

How did it go?
Awesome! I played better than I expected!

Will I get the job?
Maybe

Will this make my career?
It'll be a part of it.

Is this a success?
Only if you learn something from it.

3

The birds sing in the new day.
If there are no longer any birds, will the new day be able to dawn?

4

Are you playing or practicing?

5

Here
Now
On this day
In this moment

Yesterday is over.
Tomorrow may never happen.

6

Passion
Is
Doing
The work!

7

Life is not a competition.
Neither is music.

8

It's a big world.
There is always someone that doesn't play or sing as well
as you.
There is always someone that plays or sings better than you.
Stay humble
and
Do the work.

9

Do what you love
and
You never have to go to work!

10

Performing the right notes and rhythms are the beginning.
The music happens beyond that.

11

Celebrate everyone's successes!
Someday, it will be your turn
and
They will celebrate with you!

12

Everyone is trying to present their best work.
Respect it.
Honor it.

13

Breathe deeply.
Think deeply.
Relax.

14

Competitions
are
a crapshoot.

Send out your best work
And
Forget about it.

If you win,
Great.

If you don't
Fine.

Send it out again!

15

You are unique.
Go practice.

16

_____

Did you do the best you could
with
what you knew at the time?

If so,
Accept it.

If not,
Learn from it.

17

The only real mistake
Is
The one you keep
Making
Over and over again.

18

Should a tiger
Behave
Like
A
Monkey
Just
To
Fit
In?

19

We are all on different paths,
Respect theirs,
Respect yours.

20
_____

What is your musical gift to the world?

21

_____

How will you share your musical gift with the world?

22
———

Counting mistakes is the function of the ego.
Learning from mistakes is the function of the spirit.

23

You can't fake musicianship.
It is an honest expression of the spirit.

24

You can't teach what you don't know.
You can't express musically what you don't understand.

25

Music is a universal language.
You can communicate with anyone
In the world.

26

What does the music need?

27

Passion = Practice

28

Let your actions speak
For your
Ambition.

29

Negative Criticism:

Can you change what has been critiqued negatively?

Should you change what has been critiqued negatively?

If not, the criticism is not about you.

30

Who would you like to thank for the gift of music?

31

What gifts has music given you?

32

Teachers show the path to where you want to go.
You are the one that must make the journey.

33

What are you trying to communicate?

34

The only person who can end your career is you.
Don't be fooled by the ego of others.

35

Listen.
Listen to other artists.
Listen to other genres.
Listen to instrumentalists.
Listen to vocal music.
Listen to nature.
Listen to life.
Listen.

36

Don't take No for an answer.
If something gets in the way of your goal,
Go over it,
under it,
through it,
Around it.
Whatever it takes.

You are the only person
Who
Can set your limits.
Don't
Let
Anyone else
Do it
For you.

38

Invent your career.

Mind.
Body.
Spirit.
Music.

40

You can always say "No."
But you can't always apply (audition)
For a particular job.
Go for it.

41

The snail will eventually get to where it is going.

42

Energy in motion.

43

How bad do you want it?
Breathe deeply.
Relax.
Keep working.

44

You are talented.
Go practice.

45

You are enough.
Go practice.

46

Every part,
Every role
Is
Important.

47

Eventually, it will be your turn.
Go practice.

48

Collaborate.
Collaborate with other musicians.
Collaborate with artists.
Collaborate with writers.
Collaborate with business people.
Collaborate with teachers.
Collaborate with scientists.
Collaborate with historians.
Collaborate with philosophers.
Collaborate with...
Collaborate.
Collaborate.

49

_____

Anger is okay.
Step away from it.
Clarify it.
Acknowledge it.
Resolve it.

50

Frustration is okay.
Step away from it.
Clarify it.
Acknowledge it.
Resolve it.

51

Take a deep breath.
Begin again.

52
_____

See the beauty in all things.

53

Invent your opportunity.

54

Don't under-estimate yourself.
Don't over-estimate yourself.
Be honest with yourself.
Even if it hurts a little.

55

What aspect of music are you are passionate about?

56

Get up,
Dust yourself off,
Try again.

57

Love.

58

Respect.
Respect yourself.
Respect other musicians.
Respect people in other musical roles.
Respect everyone around you.
Respect.

59

See everyone's uniqueness.
See everyone's beauty.
Smile.

60

Explore.

61

Walk gently upon this earth.

62

Imagine.

63

Create.

64

Control what you can.
Let the rest go.

65

Be Kind.
Everyone has a bad day.

66

The compliment you give someone today
May be
Their turning point.

67

Am I ever going to use this information?
I don't know.

68

Laugh.

69

Learning doesn't have to be difficult.
Relax.
Do the work.

70

Improvise on
The music
You are
Practicing.

71

Spend some time with musicians in
Another musical field.

72

How good do you want to be?

73

Life is improvisation.

74

Only the brave...

75
_____

How did it feel when you played your best?

76

What are your fears?

77

Play fast passages quickly,
But never hurry.

78

Every day is a gift.

79

Fear of failure
Often
makes
failure
more
likely.

80

Setbacks
Are
Opportunities
For
Comebacks.

81

Confidence
Comes
From
Preparation.

82

Fear
Often
Leads
To
Over-control.

83

No Risk.
No Magic.

84

Focus on making the music,
Not just the notes.

85

Less Fear.
Less Tension.

86

Focus on what you want to happen,
Not what you don't want to happen.

87
_____

Believe in yourself.
It is no one else's job to affirm your ability.

88

What are your distractions?

89

The world is not black and white.
Neither is life.

90

Refuse to quit.

91

Can you hear the silence between the notes?

92

Deep
Desire

93

Discipline
Determination

94

What is the composer communicating to the audience
Through you?

95

Be an optimist.

96

Give yourself
permission.

97

Let it go...

98

What did you accomplish today?

99

Best Effort = Success

100

Forget about the goal,
Focus on the music.

101

Be courageous.
Go Practice.

102

It is a privilege to make music
With the people
You are performing with.

103

Focus on the music.

104

Are the flowers afraid to bloom?

105

You are a musician
Because
You
Can be no other.

106

How many ways can you play one note?

107

I think I can.
I think I can.
I know I can.

108

Life isn't fair.
Go Practice.

109

It takes courage to create.

110

Sing joyously!

111

Don't quit.
Go Practice.

112

Go make your own luck.

113

The perfect job
Is the job you love
Doing the Most.

114

The audience must
Know
that
Your favorite piece
Is the
Piece
You are perfoming
Right Now.

115

Be obsessive about your art.
It's okay.

116

When your soul hurts . . . .create.
When your soul is joyous . . . create.
When you're in doubt . . . create.

What is the lesson I am supposed to learn from this?

118

No pain, no gain.
Sometimes.
Be careful.

119

Uniformity
Creates
Monotony.

Lack of precision
Creates
Confusion.

120

How many different ways can you play that passage?

121

It is not only what you say,
But how you say it.

122

Each repetition must
Represent
Something different
Than the one
That came before it.

123

Sit back.
Breathe deeply.
Visualize your most successful musical moments.

124

Positive Self-talk.

125

Dreams are the seeds of greatness.
Work is the soil in which they grow.

126

You can be great at one,
Maybe two things.
Everything else is secondary.

127

How are you breathing?

128

Improvement
Is
A
Day by day
Activity.

129

Preparation = Confidence

130

How can you play a sound
So profoundly
That makes
The audience
Cry?

131

You've been given
A gift.
Go Practice.

132

You are your own
Best
Teacher.

133

Always do your best.
Always be kind.

134

Let Yourself
Get caught up in
The music making
Experience.

135

Confidence is a self-fulfilling prophecy.

136

Integrity is everything.

Tap into the flow of the music.

138

Great music making is a balance of
Emotion
And
Discipline.

139

Prepare to practice.

140

Technique should always be
In service to the musical idea.

141

The greater your technique,
The greater your expressive possibilities.

142

There is always another way to get where you want to go.

143

Life is full of detours.
Just keep going in the direction
You need to go in.

144
_____

Always
Open yourself up
To
The
Musical experience.

145

Trust yourself.

146

Make Friends
With
People
In other
Disciplines.

147

Musicians are social creatures.
Unplug.

Uplift
The
Musicians
Next
To you.

149

Help yourself out,
Share the gift
Of music
With
Someone Younger
Than
You.

150

Dance to the music
And then
Play the music.

151

Go Practice.

ABOUT THE AUTHOR

Amy Dunker is a Professor of Music at Clarke University where she teaches music theory, aural skills, composition and trumpet. She also directs the new music and free improvisation ensembles. Amy has a DMA in Composition from the University of Missouri–Kansas City Conservatory of Music, MM in Composition from Butler University, MM in Trumpet Performance from the University of South Dakota and a BME in Music Education from Morningside College. Amy has given masterclasses and performances in the United States, Mexico, Brazil, Colombia, Ecuador and the Czech Republic. She has presented at the International Trumpet Guild Conference, College Music Society Conferences, National Association of Schools of Music Conference (NASM), Society of Composers, Inc., Conferences as well as others. Her works have been performed throughout the United States, Italy, France, Great Britain, Germany, the Ukraine, Puerto Rico, the Czech Republic, Mexico, China, Colombia, Ecuador, Argentina, Brazil, the Republic of Georgia, Thailand and India. Her works have been recorded by the Kuhn Choir (Czech Republic), the Czech Radio Orchestra, Jaime Guiscafre (Guitar), Paata Beridze (Trumpet), Adam Hayes (Trumpet) and Kris Carlisle (Piano). Her work "Julien's Dream" will be recorded by the University of Nebraska-Omaha Symphonic Wind Ensemble under the direction of Karen Fanin in December, 2019 as part of the "… and we were heard" project. Her works are published by Alliance Publications, Inc.

Made in the USA
San Bernardino, CA
18 November 2019